15.33

HESSTON PUBLIC LIBRARY
110 E. SMITH
P.O. BOX 640
HESSTON, KANSAS 67062

HESSTON PUBLIC LIBRARY
T 23979

WITHDRAWN

The Turtle

This book has been reviewed
for accuracy by
David Skryja
Associate Professor of Biology
University of Wisconsin Center—Waukesha.

Library of Congress Cataloging in Publication Data

Oda, Hidetomo.
　　The turtle.

　　(Nature close-ups)
　　Translation of: Kame / text by Hidetomo Oda,
photographs by Hidekazu Kubo.
　　Summary: Discusses the life cycle, behavior patterns,
and habitats of various kinds of turtles.
　　1. Turtles—Juvenile literature. [1. Turtles]
I. Kubo, Hidekazu, ill. II. Title. III. Series.
QL666.C503313　1986　　　597.92　　　85-28234
ISBN 0-8172-2547-1 (lib. bdg.)
ISBN 0-8172-2572-2 (softcover)

This edition first published in 1986 by Raintree Publishers Inc.

Text copyright © 1986 by Raintree Publishers Inc., translated from
Tortoises copyright © 1979 by Jun Nanao and Hidetomo Oda.

Photographs copyright © 1979 by Hidekazu Kubo.

World English translation rights for *Color Photo Books on Nature*
arranged with Kaisei-Sha through Japan Foreign-Rights Center.

All rights reserved. No part of this book may be reproduced or utilized
in any form or by any means, electronic or mechanical, including
photocopying, recording, or by any information storage and retrieval
system, without permission in writing from the Publisher. Inquiries
should be addressed to Raintree Publishers Inc., 310 W. Wisconsin
Avenue, Milwaukee, Wisconsin 53203.

2 3 4 5 6 7 8 9 0　　　90 89 88 87

The Turtle

Raintree Publishers
Milwaukee

◀ **A turtle swimming.**

This freshwater turtle lives in rivers and ponds in Japan. The *Clemmys japonica* is a popular species sold in pet stores there.

▶ **A mother turtle and her babies.**

This species of turtle, *Geoclemys reevesii*, gives off a bad odor when it is disturbed. The color and pattern of its shell make it easily distinguishable from other types of turtles.

Turtles have existed for about 200 million years—even before dinosaurs lived on the earth! Today, there are about 240 kinds, or species, of turtles in the world. Some live on land, some live in the sea, some live in freshwater ponds and rivers. Some species are smaller than a mouse. Others weigh almost a ton!

The turtle belongs to a class of animals called reptiles. Reptiles were among the first animals to leave the sea and adapt to living on the land, millions of years ago. Crocodiles, snakes, and lizards are also reptiles. Although the turtle has many things in common with other reptiles, one feature sets it apart—its shell. All turtles have shells, whether they are plain dull brown or black, spotted, striped, or blotched with bright colors.

◀ **An adult turtle waking from hibernation.**

When it wakes from hibernation, this turtle will lift its heavy shell and set off slowly for its home territory, a large pond. There it will catch food and bask in the warm sunlight.

▶ **A turtle searching for food.**

As the weather gets warmer, the turtle becomes more active and crawls around on the bottom of the pond, looking for food. Scientists believe each adult turtle has its own territory in a pond or river.

Reptiles are cold-blooded animals. That means that their body temperature changes with the temperature of the air. So, when it becomes very cold in winter, the turtle's body functions slow down, and it hibernates. Some freshwater turtles hibernate by burrowing into the warm, muddy bottom of a pond or stream. Some crawl into the earth, burrowing beneath leaves and dry grass. In cold climates, a turtle may go into hibernation in October and not wake up until the weather begins to warm up in April or May.

When it first wakes up, the turtle moves very slowly and rests a great deal in the sun in order to raise its body temperature.

▲ A pond in springtime.

◀ **A turtle eating a crayfish.**

A turtle's diet varies from species to species. Some eat only meat. Some eat only plants. But many kinds, like this pond turtle, eat both plants and animals.

The adult pond turtle looks sluggish on land. But in the water it moves quickly and easily. It chases small fish or crayfish and, stretching out its neck, quickly seizes its victim, or prey. Turtles have no teeth. But they have a strong beak, and their upper and lower jaws have a hard edge used for biting. The turtle uses the claws on its front feet to tear its food into pieces.

The adult female turtle eats a great deal in early summer, before the mating season, so that the eggs she carries inside her body can develop.

▼ **A turtle catching a fish.** The turtle feeds on fish, crayfish, shrimps, and water insects. It helps keep the pond clean by eating dead animals.

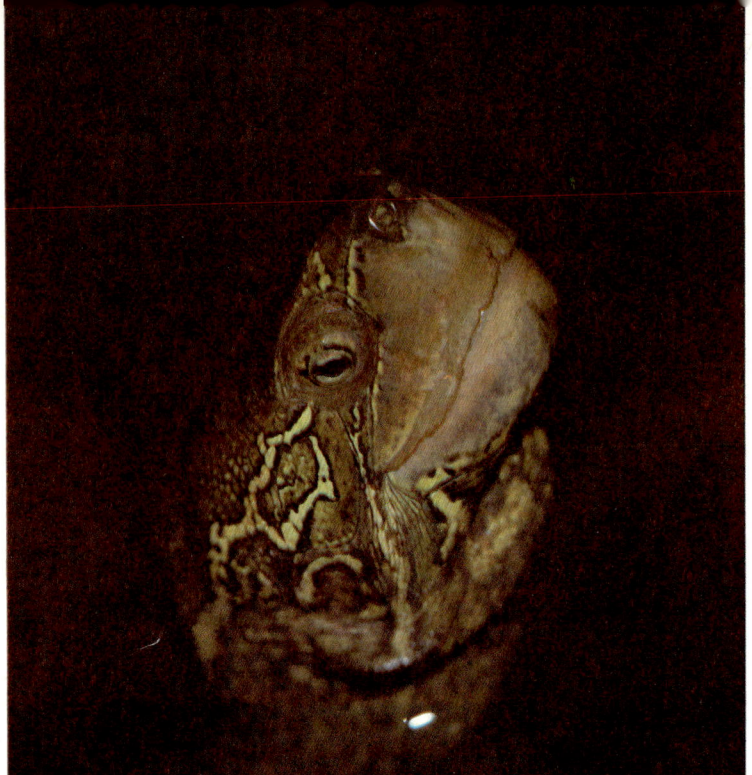

◀ **A turtle breathing out of water.**

All reptiles breathe air with their lungs. So turtles cannot breathe underwater, as fish do with their gills. Turtles must come to the surface of the pond for air now and then.

The turtle's hard shell is its unique feature. It was originally developed to protect its body from drying out in the sun millions of years ago, when the turtle first left the sea to live on land. The top part of the shell, which covers the turtle's back, is called the carapace. The part that covers its underside, or belly, is called the plastron.

The shell also protects the turtle, almost like a suit of armor. When a turtle senses danger, it pulls its head and legs safely inside its shell and hides.

◀ **A male and female turtle.**

In this species of turtle (*Geoclemys reevesii*), one can tell the male from the female by the different colors of their heads. The male's head (left) is dull and unmarked. The female's (right) has yellow markings.

▼ **Turtle basking in the sun.** Every day, this pond turtle crawls out of the water and sunbathes. The warm sunlight prevents mold and algae from growing on the shell and keeps it healthy. The turtle basks in the sun until its shell is dry and turns a whitish color.

◀ **A turtle begins her journey.**

Some kinds of turtles come out of the water several times a year to lay eggs. Most turtles lay their eggs between late spring and early fall.

▶ **A turtle on her night journey.**

Many turtles lose their lives on their dangerous journey to lay eggs. They may be run over by cars or attacked by other animals.

All species of turtles, including freshwater and sea turtles, climb onto dry land to lay their eggs. One evening in June, after mating, this female pond turtle crawls up out of the water. For two or three days, she stays near the pond's edge, looking around her, waiting for a fine evening to start her journey inland.

Then the turtle sets off, pushing her way through undergrowth, crawling over stony paths and across wide fields. She travels at night when it is cool, and when the darkness hides her from natural enemies, or predators. She may travel half a mile or more in her search for just the right spot to lay her eggs. She looks for dry clay earth in a place where the sun will shine brightly.

◀ **A turtle journeying across a field.**

When the turtle leaves the pond or river, she travels a long way inland to lay her eggs, as her ancestors have done.

The turtle's journey to lay eggs is dangerous. She could be eaten by a natural predator. Or the hot sun could dry out her body. So she must travel at night or during the coolest of the daytime hours. It may take her three or four days to find a place to lay her eggs. The trip she makes instinctively is the same trip turtles have been making for millions of years. This instinct is so strong that some species of sea turtles swim thousands of miles to nest at the same beach where they were hatched.

▼ **A turtle resting in the shade.**

During the heat of midday, the turtle stops to rest in the shade. If the air temperature rises above 35° Celsius (95° F), the turtle could easily die from the heat.

◀ **A female turtle with moist eyes.**

As she digs the hole for her eggs, the turtle's head is hidden in the undergrowth and her eyes are filled with tears. The tears protect her eyes from dryness.

▶ **A turtle laying her eggs.**

The turtle lays her eggs through an ovipositor at the base of her tail. These eggs are a little over an inch long.

After finding a place to lay her eggs, the turtle waits until nightfall before starting to dig a hole. She breaks up the ground with her claws and scrapes away the earth with her hind legs, using them like a shovel. As she digs, she urinates on the earth to moisten and soften it. After digging the hole, she stops to rest. Then she lays her first white egg. This species of pond turtle lays from ten to twenty eggs at one time. Other species may lay as few as one or as many as two hundred eggs.

▲ **A turtle digging her hole.**

As she breaks up the ground with her claws and urinates to soften it, the turtle presses down the moist earth to keep the sides of the hole from falling in. When completed, this hole will be about five inches deep and three inches wide.

▲ **A turtle hiding her nest.**
The covered nest helps to protect the turtle eggs from predators and bad weather.

▲ **A nest filled with eggs.**
The turtle's nest must be deep enough so that the eggs stay moist and are at the right temperature. This is so the baby turtles can develop properly.

The white turtle eggs are strong and do not break as they are deposited in the hole. After laying each egg, the mother turtle carefully arranges it in the nest with her hind legs. When all the eggs have been laid, the turtle uses her hind legs to spread earth over the nest to hide it. The smell of urine in the soil is a sign to other turtles not to dig in the same place. But the odor may also attract animals, such as weasels and snakes, who like to eat turtle eggs.

When the turtle's task is completed, she makes the long journey back to the pond, and the eggs are left to develop on their own.

▼ **The turtle returns to the pond after laying her eggs.**

Not all turtles return safely to the pond. Many are run over by cars or are attacked by predators. But year after year, the surviving turtles repeat the same dangerous journey to lay their eggs.

▲ A young turtle breaking its shell.

The baby turtle first makes a small hole in the eggshell with the sharp bump, or egg tooth, on the end of its nose. Then, using the claws on its front feet, it enlarges the hole.

▲ The turtle's head appears.

The yellow markings on this baby turtle's head are just like its mother's. The white bump at the tip of its nose is the egg tooth.

The strong sun warms the eggs in the earth and the young turtle embryos begin to develop. Each embryo feeds on the nutritious egg yolk which surrounds it. Within a few days, the embryo's tiny heart begins to beat, and blood flows through its veins. As the turtle develops, its ribs and backbone move to the outside of its body, forming the turtle's shell. Two or three months after an egg is laid, the baby turtle is ready to hatch.

◀ A young turtle inside its egg.

The sac of yolk (arrow) still surrounds this turtle, which will hatch in a few days. After it is born, the remainder of the yolk sac will be absorbed into its body through a small hole in the turtle's lower shell.

▼ **A young turtle crawling out of its shell.** Except for its tiny size and large head, the newborn turtle looks like an adult. But the baby's shell is still soft enough to be easily dented.

◀ **Young turtles in the nest.**

Turtles that hatch in autumn might not leave the nest until springtime. Many species hibernate through the cold winter, protected below the ground from the cold. The hibernating babies live on stored energy.

Because the eggs were all laid at once, they will hatch at the same time. These young turtles are only a little over an inch long when they first hatch. As they move about in the nest, getting the feel of their legs, the walls of the nest begin to crumble. When it rains and the ground becomes soft, the young turtles dig their way to the earth's surface.

▲ **A young turtle peeps out of the ground.**

When it rains, the earth becomes soft and the young turtles are able to dig their way out of the nest.

▲ **A young turtle crawls out of its nest.**

The young turtles crawl out of the nest at night, under cover of darkness. After looking around, each turtle sets out on its own.

▼ **A young turtle journeys to water.** Once the young turtles have left the nest, they part company. Each turtle instinctively begins its own journey to find water.

◀ **A young turtle crossing a parched field.**

After crawling through the jungle of grass that towers above it, this turtle must cross a seemingly endless, dry field. Here, in plain view, it is easy prey to hawks, snakes, and other predators.

▶ **A young turtle in a puddle.**

In the heat of the day, this young turtle crawls into a mud puddle to cool off.

Millions of years after the first turtles came up on land, some turtles adapted once again to life in the water. So, just as its ancestors have done, the newly hatched pond turtle sets out to find a river or pond. The tiny turtle's journey is a dangerous one. Snakes lie in wait for it in grassy fields, and crows and hawks swoop down from the sky, searching for small, slow-moving creatures to attack. Many young turtles die before they can reach water.

The young turtle lives for a while in wet bogs or shallow streams. There it feeds on tadpoles, water insects, and on the dead bodies of small creatures that float along the banks.

When it has grown bigger, the turtle moves from shallow water to the deep part of a large pond or river where there are safe places to hide and plenty of food. While many turtles live their entire lives within a few miles of where they were hatched, others make their way to new habitats far away—so that not too many turtles establish their territory in the same stretch of water. Once the turtle finds a suitable habitat, it may live in the same place for decades.

◀ **A young turtle swimming.**

The young pond turtle swims by moving its legs in dog-paddle fashion. Now and then, it sticks its head out of the water to breathe.

▶ **A water beetle eating a dead turtle.**

Water beetles, crayfish, and other pond animals feed on dead turtles.

◀ **A three-year-old turtle moves to a new home.**

This young turtle travels through a dry field as it looks for a new habitat. As a young turtle grows, it looks for a larger, deeper stretch of water where there is plenty of food.

▶ **An adult turtle swimming on the bottom of a pond.**

A large turtle has settled down in this wide, old pond as if it were the owner. Turtles live for decades in the same pond if the environment remains favorable.

Although it takes some turtles ten years to reach full growth, this species is full size by the time it is five. It has a shell that is about a foot long. It is mature enough to mate and lay eggs. So the turtle will soon make its own long journey inland.

Many reptiles live for a long time, and turtles are among the most long-lived. Some species live more than one hundred years. But recently, the long life of the turtle has been threatened by water pollution and the reclamation of ponds and lakes for development. The population of both adult and young turtles seems to be decreasing, due to the steady destruction of the turtle's habitat.

▲ Turtles live for many years in large ponds such as this one.

Let's Find Out

Where Do Land Turtles Live?

(1) A baby pond turtle, the *Trionyx sinensis*, swimming with large, webbed feet. (2) A Japanese land turtle, the *Cyclemys flavomarginata*. When it is upside down, it looks like a closed box. (3) A young green turtle, a species found in Africa.

There are many different species of turtles throughout the world. The species discussed in this book, *Geoclemys reevesii*, lives in rivers, ponds, and marshlands in Japan.

In southern Japan, there are two species of land turtles that never go into the water. They live in mountains and forests, feeding on plants and insects. Some people call turtles which live only on land *tortoises*.

And some species, like spotted turtles and bog turtles, which live part of their lives on land and part in the water, are called *semiterrestrial*.

Raising a Turtle.

Fill a Container with Water and Earth.

A young turtle should be kept in a container with enough water to almost cover its shell. There should also be a mound of dirt so the turtle can bask in the sun for short periods of time. There should also be rocks or pieces of tile under which it can hide.

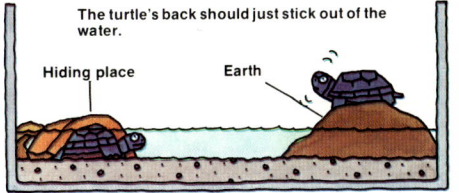
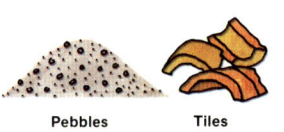

A turtle sunbathing on dry land.

Changing the Water and Feeding the Turtle.

Turtles should be fed raw fish, liver, hamburger or other lean meats. Cut the food into small pieces and feed the turtle every other day. Also, change the water every other day. It is all right to use tap water.

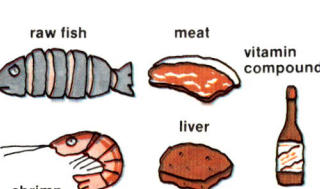

A young turtle feeding.

What to Do When Your Turtle Gets Sick.

When turtles get sick, it is usually from a vitamin deficiency. To cure your turtle, mix calcium and vitamin compound into its food. You can also add small amounts of cod liver oil.

A turtle hibernating in dried grass.

GLOSSARY

carapace—the upper shell that covers the turtle's back. (p. 10)

cold-blooded animals—animals whose temperature changes with the temperature of the air. (p. 6)

egg tooth—a sharp bump at the end of the baby turtle's nose, which is used for breaking through the eggshell. (p. 20)

embryo—the early stages of development of a turtle or other organisms. (p. 20)

hibernation—a period of inactivity undergone by animals during cold weather when their body functions slow down. (pp. 6, 22)

instinct—behavior with which an animal is born, rather than behavior which is learned. (pp. 15, 23)

ovipositor—the egg-laying organ at the base of the turtle's tail. (p. 16)

plastron—the lower shell that covers the turtle's underside. (p. 10)

predators—animals that hunt or kill other animals for food. (pp. 15, 19)

reptiles—a class of cold-blooded animals that have backbones and that usually have scaly skin and lay their eggs out of water. (pp. 4, 6, 28)

species—a group of animals which scientists have identified as having common traits. (pp. 4, 10, 12)